Purpose

The Reason for Your Existence

Jarrod Dunn

Jarrod Dunn
adamwhereareyou@yahoo.com
www.jarroddunn.com

Limits of Liability and Disclaimer of Warranty

The author and publisher shall not be liable for your misuse of this material. This book is strictly for informational and educational purposes.

Warning – Disclaimer

The purpose of this book is to educate and encourage. The author and publisher do not guarantee anyone following these techniques, suggestions, tips, ideas, or strategies will become successful. The author and publisher shall have neither liability nor responsibility to anyone with respect to any loss or damage caused or alleged to be caused, directly or indirectly by the information contained in this book.

ISBN 978-1-941749-25-8

4-P Publishing Chattanooga, TN

Printed in the United States of America

ISBN 978-1-941749-25-8

4-P Publishing

Chattanooga, TN 37411

Acknowledgments/Dedication

I would like to dedicate this book to Dr. David Banks. You came into my life at a crucial time. I was at a point where I was still trying to figure out the aspects of who, what, and why of my life. My life changed the very moment you began to teach me about purpose. I thank you so much for seeing the potential in me. I also thank you for not allowing me to be like anyone else. Thank you, Daddy Banks.

About the Author

Jarrod Dunn lives in Athens, Tennessee with his beautiful wife and four children. He is a certified Purpose, Life and Transformation coach. He is  also a businessman and the author of *"Adam Where Are You?"* Jarrod has a passion to see people in general walk in their purpose so that they may live a life that is fulfilling.

Through life experiences and training, he has been equipped with the necessary tools that are needed to help people walk with a purpose and pursue their passion.

Contents

Introduction

"The moment I realized that I had a purpose, my life changed."

-Jarrod Dunn

We are in some trying and perplexing times. When a person turns on the television, reads a newspaper or magazine the media is scattered with confusing and frustrating issues. It would seem like someone could answer the questions to the chaos, or put a stop to the madness many people experience in their lives, families, communities, and nations.

There was a time where it seemed humanity as a whole was progressing from past scars and emotional trauma, but now that progress must be seriously questioned. Facebook bombards us with images of young children disrespecting their elders. Television shows have replaced morality for immorality. Education has lost its weight in certain communities. Relationships are based on how you make the other person feel instead of "is this person beneficial to and for me". There was a period when people understood what they were doing and why they were doing it.

What is the answer to all the madness we see going on? Can the problems we experience daily be fixed or do we just have to live with them? I believe we have an answer.

In this book, *Purpose - The Reason for Your Existence*, it is my goal to offer a solution to the problems many individuals, communities, and nations wrestle.

This book answers the historical questions that have entered into the minds of mankind for many years. Questions such as: "What is my purpose?" "Why was I created?" "Was I a mistake?"

Get ready to go on a journey as we explore the answers to some of the questions that have left us confused for years.

1

What is Purpose?

"When the purpose is not known, abuse is inevitable."
— Myles Munroe, Understanding the Purpose and Power of Woman

I believe the subject of purpose is one many are looking to explore in depth. This understanding of purpose came to me one day while engaged in a conversation with a man about my life. During the conversation, a question came up about how I made the transition from one phase of my life to the next phase? I pondered the question, and I came to the conclusion that a significant part of it was discovering my purpose.

Purpose is simply defined as the reason something exists.

Many people find it hard to believe that when the God created us it was on purpose. Purpose was always in the mind of God, since the beginning of creation. Genesis 1:26 says, "And God said, Let us make man in our image, after our likeness: and let them have dominion over the fish of the sea, and over the fowl of the air, and over the cattle, and over all the earth, and over every creeping thing that creepeth upon the earth."

The text is very interesting because it gives us the account of the Creator giving rise to mankind. He creates man and gives him an assignment on what he is supposed to do while he is here on earth. He tells mankind to have dominion or rule over the fish of the sea, fowls of the air, cattle, and every creeping thing that creeps upon the earth. The scripture gives us a glimpse inside the mind of God. It shows us God never created any of us just to take up a place or occupy space in a certain location.

It must be noted when God named the animals, He also designated the location in which each animal should live. He never created the materials and allowed the materials to decide what's best for them. As we see in the scripture, God created the animals and placed them strategically in the right location. If

> *When purpose is not known abuse is inevitable. When a person does not understand the purpose of a thing, they are guaranteed to misuse it.*

one takes a fish out of the water, it will flop and eventually die. If a bird is taken out of the air, it will wander aimlessly throughout the earth. If the purpose is taken away from humanity, they will kill other human beings, abuse themselves with drugs, and give their bodies to other individuals for satisfaction at a cheap rate.

When the purpose is not known, abuse is inevitable. When a person does not understand the purpose of a thing, they are guaranteed to misuse it.

In our society today we see many things falling apart. I believe the answer to the question so many ask can be traced back to the purpose. Everything God created has been created for and with a purpose.

Modern Issues

Let's explore the purpose of a few of our modern issues.

Marriage

Marriage is a sad topic in our generation today. Many people are entering into marriage or have been married without a clue of the purpose of marriage. I can't number the conversations I have had with others who have entered into marriage on the foundation of sex, money, and emotions. It wasn't long before they found out those things weren't the right foundation to build upon.

Let me give you a few examples of what the purpose of marriage is.

1. Reflect the image of Christ

Marriage is a beautiful picture of the relationship between Christ and His church.

The bodies of believers that make up the church are collectively called the "bride" of Christ. As a bridegroom, Jesus gave His life for His bride, "to make her holy, cleansing her by the washing with water through the word." (Ephesians 5:25-26)

2. Unite

Marriage is to spiritually, emotionally and physically unite a man and a woman together, as husband and wife, in a covenantal relationship between themselves and their Creator

It is evident that sex was not the purpose of marriage. Sex is a benefit of marriage, therefore, you cannot enter marriage with the foundation of sex. The house will fall every time.

Relationships

In our society today, we treat a relationship like a piece of clothing, i.e., something to put on and throw off. For us to understand what a relationship is, we must first look and define the term.

The word relationship comes from two words, relation, and ship. The term relation according to freedictionary.com means:

1. *A logical or natural association between two or more things; relevance of one to another; connection.*

The definition of Ship from the free dictionary reads

1. *A sailing vessel having three or more square-rigged masts*

If we look at the two definitions, we see a relation is a connection between two or more people. A ship is a means of transportation.

Every relationship, mentorship, headship, and leadership was designed to sail into an important destination. If you are in a relationship and it isn't going anywhere, you have to reexamine the purpose of it.

Education

When I was a child, I would hear people say, "What you don't know won't hurt you." It was years later, I realized that cliché was far from the truth.

I grew up in a culture where education wasn't a big issue. The atmosphere I was reared in placed extracurricular activities above education. When the time had passed, and one could no longer compete or had exhausted all the options people would say, "Get a job. A hard working man who raises his family is the key to life" It wasn't until I experienced life a little I realized those who had the knowledge and could think would far surpass those who could only work with their hand. No matter how hard he or she worked.

> *"He, who opens a school door, closes a prison".*
> *This quote was so relevant because I now realize education unlocks opportunities.*

I read a quote one day by Victor Hugo while I was working on my computer that says, "He, who opens a school door, closes a prison." This quote was so relevant because I now realize education unlocks opportunities.

The late Martian Luther King Jr. stated:

> *"Education must enable a man to become more efficient, to achieve with increasing facility the legitimate goals of his life. Education must also train one for quick, resolute and effective thinking. To think incisively and to think for one's self is very difficult. We are prone to let our mental life become invaded by legions of half-truths, prejudices, and propaganda. At this point, I often wonder whether or not education is fulfilling its purpose. A great majority of the so-called educated people do not think logically and scientifically. Even the press, the classroom, the platform, and the pulpit in many instances do not give us objective and unbiased truths. To save man from the morass of propaganda, in my opinion, is one of the chief aims of education. Education must enable one to sift and weigh evidence, to discern the true from the false, the real from the unreal, and the facts from the fiction."*

These are just a few areas where purpose is relevant.

2

Born with Purpose

"You were born with a purpose and on purpose."
-anonymous

I've conversed with many people about the topic of purpose. Often the conversation has left me in amazement. I've talked to many people, and some of them have told me they think their life is a mistake. They try to justify this by comparing it to all the trials and tribulation they have encountered in life. Sadly, they have concluded the reason for all the nonsense in their life is their existence.

God never created anything without a purpose. You were born with a purpose and on purpose. I received this enlightenment one day when I was listening to one of my favorite teachers lecture on life. He began to explain the process taken when a sperm is released. He said a healthy adult male can release between 40 million and 1.2 billion sperm cells at once. When they are released every cell immediately rushes to the fertile egg. He explained that out of all the sperms released only one made it and that one was you. I thought to myself, "Wow!" that's not a coincidence, that's divine purpose.

> *Our trials and tribulations don't determine whether or not we have purpose.*

That revelation allowed me to realize that regardless of how you were born you were born with a purpose. It also helped me to understand our trials and tribulations don't determine whether or not we have a purpose.

God never made a mistake. When God created you, He knew exactly what He was doing.

As I stated earlier, the purpose is the reason for your existence. In other words, God knew exactly why He created you. There was something on planet earth that can only be solved by you, so in return He gave you as a solution to that problem. It's important we realize, God never created anything without knowing what it will become later. He always had in mind the reason for a creation.

Ephesians 2:10 says, "For we are his workmanship, created in Christ Jesus unto good works, which God hath before ordained that we should walk in them." According to the Strong's Concordance, the term "workmanship" means a *product*. This scripture illustrates God being like a manufacturer who produces a product, but not just any product, something that is of beauty.

When a manufacturer produces a product, he already has in mind the purpose of the product. One of the purposes of the product is it be a success. Let's explore the mind of a manufacturer.

Success

Success is always in the mind of the manufacturer. Let's evaluate this statement. We are in a technology age where many of us carry, or have inside our homes products manufactured by Apple. Everything Apple produces rests upon the logo on the product. The logo is the reputation of the company.

Suppose you were to order an iPhone 6 from Apple. When the product arrives at your location, it will come in a box from the company. When you open the box, the first thing you may come in contact with is a manual. The manual is nothing more than the instructions for the product. It informs you how the product operates. It gives the what, how, and why of the product. There is a section that tells you the do's and do nots of the product in the booklet. It also tells us if the product malfunctions, not to try fix it ourselves. The manual provides us with instructions where to send the product back at no cost. The reason we can ship the product back to the company at no expense because the reputation of the company is on the line. The company believes in the success of the product so much it is willing to sacrifice whatever it needs for you to be satisfied with the product.

This same illustration holds true with God. God had success in the mind for all of his creation. To show you this is true, let's look at the creative story of mankind.

Geneses 1:26 say's "And God said, Let us make man in our *image*, after our likeness…"

In the creative process of mankind the first thing God did when he created his product was to stamp it with his logo, Geneses 1:26 Say's "And God said, Let us make man in our image. The very fact we have been stamped in the image of God is an

> *Many of us do not read the manual, and in return, so many of us are receiving minimum results.*

indication success was always in the mind of God when he created us. You may be in a situation right now where it looks like your life is a failure. The very fact you have been stamped with the image of God allows me to say, I have Good News, "You haven't failed because failing isn't an option when it comes to your life.

God's image is his reputation because that is who he is. Everything God does rests upon who he is. God doesn't mind putting His reputation on the line because he cannot fail.

To determine our success God gave us a manual. The manual given to us is the Hebrew text called the Bible. Remember what I said earlier the manual serves a great purpose as it pertains to the product. It gives us an understanding of the function of the product. Sadly, many of us do not read the manual, and in return, so many of us are receiving minimum results.

Car Salesperson

I was working at a car lot one day, and we received some new Nissan Maximas. One of the rituals of the company is when a new car comes in; a more seasoned car salesperson will take a new car salesperson out to the car and do what is called a walk around. A walk around is when a car salesperson walks around the car and explains the various functions of the car; for the sole purpose of giving the less experienced colleague knowledge needed about the product.

When we were at the point of the presentation, the salesperson lifted the hood of the car, and I noticed something I immediately wanted to ask. I asked him, "Why are the newer cars being made with plastic over the engines now?" He said, "Good question." He explained, that the newer cars are coming with plastic over the engine and other parts of the car because the factory wants to protect and send a warning to people not to fix the vehicles themselves.

This explanation immediately had me thinking about the manual we have been given. It also sent a message to protect us by allowing us to know people can't fix themselves only our manufacturer can. Let me explain.

People can only assist in helping each other make the right or wrong decisions but in reality, the one who has created us has the knowledge and wisdom that enables us to function properly. The great thing about it is it is all in the manual.

3

The Importance of Purpose

"A person who doesn't walk with purpose is walking purposelessly."
-Jarrod Dunn

U nderstanding your purpose is very vital. A person who doesn't understand their purpose is a person who is living purposelessly.

10 Facts About Purpose

- Purpose is the reason for your existence
- God created you on purpose
- Purpose is an important key to your success
- Purpose is a motivational factor for focus
- Purpose allows you to be fulfilled
- When purpose is not known, abuse is inevitable
- Lack of purpose results in experimentation
- Purpose determines your value
- Purpose is more important than your past

I've encountered many conversations with individuals who have asked me the question, "How did you make the transition from one lifestyle to another?"

I never really wanted to make the answer to the question so spiritual that others couldn't comprehend what I was saying. So many times we can be so caught up in being deep that people drown trying to figure out what we're saying.

In life, many people are inspired by various things. Some can be motivated by the writings of philosophers. Others can be stirred by the activities of authority figures.

In my case, I have been inspired by the ancient Hebrew scrolls called the Bible. In this so-called antiquated book, I have found some great principles that have truly impacted my life.

In the writings of the Bible, I have found two things that stand out to me: one, the person of Jesus, who prepared us for eternity, and two, the principles of Jesus which equips us for now.

> *The person who doesn't understand everything has a purpose, is someone who will continue to go through life experimenting. They will experiment with relationships, education, physical health, and most importantly life.*

The person of Jesus has allowed me to change because He has extended His Grace for my life. The grace of God has allowed me to be forgiven, now and in the life to come.

The principles of Jesus has equipped me with the knowledge to know I have been created with, and on, purpose. The moment I received the revelation I had a purpose, my whole outlook on life changed.

The person who doesn't understand that everything has a purpose is someone who will continue to go through life experimenting. They will experiment with relationships, education, physical health, and most importantly life.

Often people make the principles of Jesus so far-fetched many give up, frustrated in the process. One thing I have learned that has helped me tremendously is we have a real God, who deals with real people. "God is relevant"!!!!

Renewing Your Mind

Understanding the importance of purpose has changed the course of my life. There was a period in my life I thought it was only by chance some succeed and others did not. Unfortunately, I felt I was in the category with those who were destined to fail, primarily due to my environment and culture. Life example and daily living had formed my thought on success.

When I began to renew my mind with the correct principles of the Bible, I began to see life in a new perspective. According to the Strong's Concordance, the word "renew" comes from a word that means to renovate. It paints a picture of one who is renovating something. If you have ever witnessed or been a part of renovating something, you know one of the things done in the process, is to take out the old to replace it with the new. The process is the same when it comes to renewing the mind. I had a belief system built on the foundation of other people's philosophy. Therefore, I had to take out the old thinking that said "You can't succeed," and "Your past mistakes are all you'll ever be in life," etc. and replace it with what God has truly purposed for me.

Your purpose will always transcend your past, present, and future mistakes. An Old Testament prophet quoted these powerful words from God, *"I make known the end from the beginning, from ancient times, what is still to come, I say, "My purpose will stand, and I will do all that I please." Isaiah 46:10*

4

How to Find Your Purpose

"The two most important days in your life are the day you are born and the day you find out why."
Mark Twain

Follow the directions on the purpose discovery worksheet provided on this page.

Purpose Discovery

Discovering yourself to achieve your purpose and unlock your potential

1. What do you see in society that burdens or grieves you?

Write down something you see around you that makes you either extremely angry or very sad. If you tolerate it, it will not cause you to do anything about it. It is when you can no longer accept it that you are prompted to do something about it.

2. What groups of people are you passionate about (Circle one)?

Circle only one group. If you find yourself wanting to impact more than one group, then circle "people in general."

People in General   Children   Couples   Teens

Professionals   Adults   Seniors   Men

Families   Religious group   Non-Christians

An ethnic group   Women   Single   Other

Single Parents

3. What would be your message to this group?

Everyone has a message. Limit your words, but think about what you would say if standing in front of the group you identified in question #2, what would you say to this group? Write it down.

4. Choose words as to how you would like to help the above group.(Circle Two)

Words are powerful. Take your time to choose TWO that will describe the impact you want to have on the group you identified in question #2.

Motivate	Create	Discover
Encourage	Comfort	Lead
Empower	Influence	Impact
Nurture	Impart	Repair
Challenge	Equip	Minister
Serve	Change	Revive

Develop   Organize   Renew   Other

5. **What do you want this above group to become as a result of your influence (Circle one)?**

After encountering you, what do you imagine this group will look like once you have impacted them with your message?

Examples:

To live a successful life

To be productive

Maximize their potential

To enjoy life

To obtain more out of their goals

Other

6. **Take the answers to the questions and follow the purpose code 4, 2, 3, 5**

(Write the answer you had for each number)

Write the answers to questions number 4, 2, 3, and 5 next to the corresponding numbers below to form the Purpose Code.

4:

2:

3:

5:

Take the answers you had for 4, 2, 3, and 5 and form a complete sentence with them. Try to minimize your words.

Example:

My Purpose is to equip and develop leaders to walk with purpose so they may live a fulfilled life.

Write YOUR purpose below

5

Activating Your Purpose

"Your purpose is the magnet that attracts opportunities."
-Jarrod Dunn

It is truly my belief God had something He wanted to do on planet earth and in oder for Him to get something accomplished He needed a physical body to achieve the goal. In return, He created you to be the agent to bring about the change. Your purpose has the potential to solve earth's problems.

3 Dimensions

Purpose has three levels:

1. Purpose Blueprint

2. Purpose Fingerprint

3. Purpose Footprint

Let's explore them one by one.

Purpose Blueprint

"The Plan"

When the universe was created, it was produced out of intention and not out of an impulse. Others have tried to discredit the creative ability of God by defining it as a mishap, mistake, or compulsion. The very first words of the ancient Hebrew text tell us, *"In the beginning, God created the heavens and the earth."* The word "created" in this script means to select, cut down, and construct. It gives a connotation of one selecting something and then picking out the material needed to build it. God started the creation process just like any great architect would do before they began to build anything with a blueprint.

The Old Testament prophet Jeremiah states what God thought about the children of Israel in the twenty-ninth chapter, eleventh verse when they weren't following the plan. He quotes *"For I know the thought that I think towards you, saith the Lord, thought of peace, and not of evil, to give you an expected end."* The word "thought" in this scripture means *plan* according to the New Strong's Exhaustive Concordance of the Bible. In essence, God was letting the children of Israel know what they were going through, at that time, was not a part of the original plan. There may be some things we go through in life that isn't part of the original blueprints God has for our lives. Keep in mind the plans God has for your life does not change.

When a builder begins to construct or create something, he has the plans or blueprint to accomplish the job.

When God began to create, He didn't create from nothing. He had the thoughts or plan already in mind. When He began to call things forth, He was just proclaiming the things that were a part of the plan.

Genesis 1:26 gives us the blueprint for humanity. It says, *"And God said, Let us make man in our image, after our likeness: and let them have dominion over the fish of the sea, and fowl of the air, and over the cattle, and over all the earth, and over every creeping thing that creepeth upon the earth."* The plan for humankind was to have dominion, but not over other people. The verse states, *"let them have dominion over the fish of the sea, and fowl of the air, and over the cattle, and over all the earth, and over every creeping thing that creepeth upon the earth."* The blueprint was to dominate the earth. The word dominion means to rule. In other words, the earth was supposed to serve us because it is under our authority or rule.

Think about the rich land of Kuwait, which has provided us with oil. Think about the gold mines of South Africa that have provided us with a wealth of resources, and all the inventions created. The cars we drive recieve their designs from the earth resources. This is a revelation you must receive. God has created mankind to rule over the earth. The earth was created to serve us with its vast resources.

Purpose Fingerprint

"The Unique Design"

God created humanity with a blueprint, but He didn't stop there. He also wanted to make sure He gave us a personal plan for our individual lives. The reason this portion is named "purpose fingerprint" is because no two people have the same fingerprints. God never does anything the same; He is too powerful for such redundancy. This is an indication God never created two people to function the same way, as it pertains to their individual purpose. God isn't looking for echoes in the earth.

Purpose fingerprint has to do with the reason for your creation. Many people are confused about their life right now because they don't understand they have been uniquely designed to be themselves. I can't help but think about the many years I spent trying to talk, walk and act, like someone I was never created to be. In return, I had to work overtime trying to impress others with someone else's gifts and talents. Don't misunderstand me, there have been some great men and women who greatly impacted my life, but at the end of the day, I was never designed to live my life mimicking them. There is nothing wrong with displaying some characteristic of those who had inspired you, but don't stop being the person you are to become someone you are not. I've gone through some gloomy days and frustrating nights in order to gain the wisdom I was supposed to learn from others but being careful not to emulate them. The world doesn't need cookie cutter people. I use this analogy because when one uses a cookie cutter, you duplicate the form of the cookie cutter in the dough. "If I stop being who I am to become you, then I'm duplicating two pieces of the puzzle that God, my family, community, and society does not need."

I think one of the greatest services we can provide to people is the ability to help them recognize their personality. You have been uniquely designed to use your gifts and talents to serve others.

Take the answer you had in chapter 4, "Purpose Discovery." This chapter should have given you some great motivation for life. In following the directions properly, you would see what you came up with is a passion that has been placed inside of you. It's also important to note if you did that chapter with a friend or family member, the two of you will have different answers. Why? Because, no two people have the same purpose.

I quoted in the earlier chapters that purpose is the reason for your existence. The answer you have come up with is one of the reasons for your creation here on the earth. You have uniquely been designed to solve a problem, or change a situation, with the very purpose instilled in you.

Have you ever wondered why there are some things in your life that burden you but do not seem to bother anyone else? That is a great indication that by implementing your purpose, you have the solution to that burden. You could very well be the answer to some business adventure or mother's prayer. The thing inside of you could be the answer to the problems a school, corporation, or family is having. Do not allow media, television, demographics, race and gender to define you and tell you that you are someone or something, other than whom and for what you have been created.

Purpose Gauge

Here's another way to get a sense of your life's purpose. Review the kind of person you are and the abilities that come naturally to you, even if such abilities have gotten you into trouble in the past, you can gain insight into your life purpose, says psychotherapist Tina Tessina, Ph.D., author of *The Ten Smartest Decisions a Woman Can Make after Forty*.

Create a list of descriptions of yourself in each of the following categories. It may be helpful if you get a separate sheet of notebook paper and pencil.

1. Personal qualities (e.g., friendly, intellectual, a good communicator)

2. Your talents (e.g., painting, motivating people by public speaking, athletics, mentoring)

3. The circumstances that tend to repeat in your life (e.g., do you wind up teaching others, listening to people's problems: or working with children or technology?)

4. Your desires (e.g., traveling, cleaning up the environment, running for political office)

Take the answer that is most important to you in each category and complete the following sentence:

I _____(your name) am designed to be a _____ (insert personal quality) who can _____ (insert talent) and I find myself _____ (fill in recurring patterns or circumstances) often, because I am supposed to _____ (desire).

Example:

I, the President of the U.S., (your name) am designed to be a good communicator (insert personal quality) who can motivate people through my speeches (insert talent) and I often find myself listening to people's problems (fill in recurring patterns or circumstances) because I am supposed to run for office and improve their circumstances (desire).

- See more at http://www.success.com/article/answer-6-questions-to-reveal-your-life-purpose#sthash.VeAeGTyX.dpuf

Purpose Footprint

"The Plan of Action"

Your purpose was never given to you for the sole purpose of you benefiting from it. In all actuality, your purpose is for the benefit of others. Once you realize your purpose it is paramount to know that it is the solution to someone's problem.

When talking about purpose, I can't help but think about a small lady by the name of Mother Teresa. Her story is amazing. She was a solution to a problem her country was experiencing.

The great civil rights leader, Martin Luther King, came on the scene during a time when segregation was common in the south. His purpose was to expose the unjust laws of the system and to let others know that regardless of one's skin color, individuals are not separate, but equal.

There have been many great men and women in our time who realized they were born for something other than service to themselves.

You were born and created to do something great. Don't waste your life doing ordinary things. It is my opinion each person is created to do the extraordinary in life. The definition of "ordinary", according to the freedictionay.com is "common, usual, not particularly good; not better than average." With this definition in mind, it would seem people have no meaning or purpose. We know that isn't true based on the evidence proven in the course of this book.

If you were to take an inventory of the locations that form a consistent pattern in your life, these locations are places you have an opportunity to allow your purpose to flourish. If we believe everything has a purpose then we must realize it is only because of purpose we are there.

In Closing

I want to summarize with this story. I was on my way to work one morning. I wanted to stay behind, so I told my wife I would go and get her breakfast when I come in. Upon my arrival, I noticed there was a young man and his dog sitting in front of my business. The scene was very alarming because the young man was poorly dressed and his dog was dressed up with make-up. I didn't want to get out of the car reacting, so I parked my car and asked the young man if he was hungry. He responded, "Yes." I went inside the building and began to pray, asking for wisdom in this situation. I came outside of the building and handed the man some food; he began to eat, sharing some of his meal with his dog. As he was eating, I began to talk to him about his purpose. I told him regardless of what he was going through and had gone through, it does not eliminate the fact he has a purpose. I told him the very reason he was there with me that day, was an indication he had a purpose.

The young man put his sandwich down and looked at me and said, "I've never heard that." We began to have a conversation about his life and what he thought had led him to that point. After we had finished talking, he got up, shook my hand and told me he wanted to see me again, and then he gave me a hug. I can't help but think for that small moment of time, that young man experienced something he had never experienced before, a "sense of purpose."

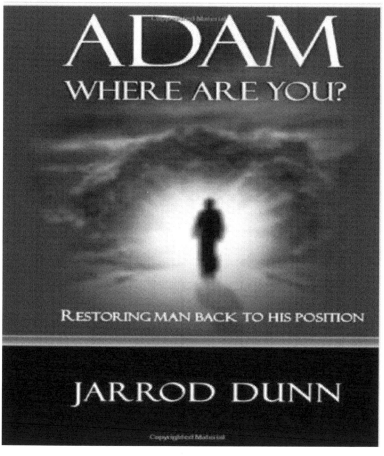

Adam, Where Are You? is a life changing, mind renewing guide for men. This book is geared to help men find their purpose, tap into their potential and walk toward destiny. It has been written with the intention of challenging and inspiring the man to reclaim what rightfully belongs to him. This is a must read book for men who are ready to bring about change in their home, community and nation.

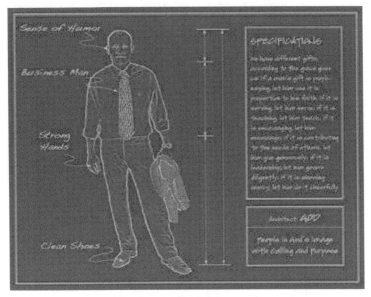

"The Blueprint"

This workshop is geared to equip and train men to understand their purpose and potential. It will also help each participant to identify their goals in life and how to pursue them.

Invasion

Invasion is a workshop that equips leaders to identify the problems within their cities and communities. The leaders will be able to create a solution to solve the problem. This workshop will allow you to become a city strategist, problem solver, and agent of change within your community.

Visit us online for seminars, workshops and other products.

Click: www.jarroddunn.com

Call 423-457-9542

Get Connected

www.jarroddunn.com

facebook/AuthorJarrodDunn

twitter/Jarrod_Dunn

Follow us on Facebook

The Joseph Project

This page is dedicated to equipping leaders to walk with purpose.

Made in the USA
Columbia, SC
08 October 2024

43233889R00035